Confronting the Idols of Our Age

Wycliffe Studies in Gospel,
Church, and Culture

———————

This series, emanating from Wycliffe College, Toronto, addresses key topics and issues in the church and in contemporary culture.

Grounded in the historic tradition of the Christian faith, the series presents topical subject matter in an accessible form and seeks to appeal to a broad audience.

Confronting the Idols of Our Age

EDITED BY
Thomas P. Power

RESOURCE *Publications* • Eugene, Oregon

CONFRONTING THE IDOLS OF OUR AGE
Wycliffe Studies in Gospel, Church, and Culture

Copyright © 2017 Wipf and Stock Publishers. All rights reserved. Except for brief quotations in critical publications or reviews, no part of this book may be reproduced in any manner without prior written permission from the publisher. Write: Permissions, Wipf and Stock Publishers, 199 W. 8th Ave., Suite 3, Eugene, OR 97401.

Resource Publications
An Imprint of Wipf and Stock Publishers
199 W. 8th Ave., Suite 3
Eugene, OR 97401

www.wipfandstock.com

PAPERBACK ISBN: 978-1-5326-0433-1
HARDCOVER ISBN: 978-1-5326-0435-5
EBOOK ISBN: 978-1-5326-0434-8

Manufactured in the U.S.A.

Contents

Preface | vii

1 Redeeming the Idols | 1
  —John Bowen

2 Hedonism | 8
  —Judy Paulsen

3 Narcissism | 15
  —Peter Robinson

4 Individualism | 19
  —David Kupp

5 Consumerism | 26
  —L. Ann Jervis

6 Omnism | 30
  —Joseph Mangina

7 Fatalism | 35
  —Christopher Seitz

8 Careerism | 39
  —Thomas Power

9 Relativism | 43
  —Marion Taylor

10 Gnosticism | 49
  —J. Glen Taylor

11 Positivism | 58
  —Alan L. Hayes

12 Reductionism | 64
  —Ephraim Radner

Bibliography | 71
List of Contributors | 73

Preface

The series entitled Wycliffe College Studies in Gospel, Church, and Culture is intended to present topical subject matter in an accessible form and seeks to appeal to a broad audience. Typically titles in the series derive from sermons given by the faculty of Wycliffe College, Toronto, in its Founders' Chapel. The current volume on confronting the different idols of our age is the first in the series and derives from a sermon series given in the Fall of 2015.

I wish to thank my fellow contributors for their willingness to contribute to the current volume. I also want to express a special thanks to Rachel Lott of Wycliffe College for her work on formatting the manuscript.

Thomas P. Power.

1

Redeeming the Idols

JOHN BOWEN

PRESIDENT CALVIN COOLIDGE WAS a man of few words. He came home from church one day and his wife asked him what the sermon had been about. He replied, "Sin." His wife (who obviously knew him well) persisted, "And what did he have to say about sin?" The president replied, "He was against it."

Jeremiah is against idolatry. But he says it with a little more passion than Calvin Coolidge. In fact, Jeremiah is absolutely boiling over with outrage. In Jeremiah 2:12 he cries out: "Be appalled, O heavens, at this, be shocked, be utterly desolate, says the Lord." To Jeremiah, this idol worship is beyond comprehension. How can you possibly do this? No other nation has done such a thing. Even though their gods are nothing, at least they're loyal! And you had so many privileges!

Who made the idols?

Idolatry: an evil thing, surely. But here is a shocking statement: an idol is actually a good thing. Why is it good? Because God created it. After all, nothing exists that God did not create and God created all things good. Thus sex can be an idol, but before it was an idol it was a good creation of God. Materialism is an idol, but to have a material world was God's idea in the first place. Workaholism is an idol, but work is itself a good gift of God.

What turns these good gifts of God into idols is what we have done with them. We have removed them from under the authority of God, where they could have been channels of God's blessing to us. We have also stopped exercising our own God-delegated authority over them—which was a part of our God-given stewardship of the world.

Instead we have put these things on a pedestal and made them into mini-gods. We have given them power over our lives that they were not created to have and which (note this) they are not capable of bearing. As Paul puts it, we "worship the creature (the created thing) instead of the Creator" (Rom 1:25). If you like, we are putting Saul's armor on David and finding that he cannot bear the weight. David is a great shepherd boy, but he is useless as a knight in shining armor.

Why do we do this foolish thing? Jeremiah pinpoints the problem in verse 20: "Long ago you broke your yoke, and burst your bonds, and you said, 'I will not serve!'" (In saying this he anticipates Milton's Satan: "Better to reign in Hell than serve in Heaven.") The first taste of this is in the garden, when the serpent promises, "You will be as gods" (Gen 3:5). You do not need God: you can be your own god. There is the first idol: us. Ultimately, that is why we like idols: because they help prop up our own idolatry and perpetuate our illusion that we are in control.

But of course, human beings are already as God-like as they are capable of being, since they are in the image of

God. God has blessed us with all the God-ness we can handle. And so, when human beings try to play God, they get into trouble because the job is way above their pay-grade.

So what is the attraction of idols? For one thing, idols are less demanding than God. They make wonderful promises: they will make you happy, they will solve your problems, and they will give your life meaning and purpose. And because God has given them only limited power—they are creatures as we are—we think they are easier to control, easier to bend to our will than Almighty God.

The trouble is that in the end our idols cannot keep their promises, and they will destroy us. As Jeremiah says, we "went after worthless things, and became worthless themselves" (2:5). If we are looking to David in Saul's armor to win our battles, the Philistines will destroy us.

Part of their destructiveness comes from the fact that we are created to become like the things we worship. We are made to worship God and to become like God. That is our high destiny. So if we worship lesser things, we will become less than God intends for us.

Jeremiah has a powerful image for all this, that of water: "My people have committed two evils: they have forsaken me, the fountain of living water, and dug out cisterns for themselves, cracked cisterns that can hold no water" (2:13). In that culture, the people would build big water-tanks to catch the rain in the rainy season, so that they would have a water supply in times of drought. So to have a leaky cistern was a disaster! No water, no life. It's as simple as that.

Rick Warren imagines it this way:

> It is like we are hopelessly lost in the desert, dying of thirst, seeking anything to quench our

> parched, dry throats. We see a kiosk with big flashing neon lights, and God is holding up a sign that says, "Living Water Available Here." Yet we say, "No, thanks, God! Appreciate the offer, but I see a shovel over there. I think I'll dig my own cistern!" Off we trot to start digging our own well and our own cistern. We abandon God who does not just have water but a spring of water that will never dry up, and we decide to figure our problem out by ourselves. The problem is that our cisterns always break; they never hold up. The water leaks out, so we remain thirsty, unable to quench our own thirst.[1]

As Jeremiah says, "In the time of their trouble they say, 'Come and save us!' But where are your gods that you made for yourself? Let them come, if they can save you, in your time of trouble" (2:27–28). The idols let us down precisely when we need them most.

Every way of life has its own distinctive temptations to idolatry. Here is an example from one world which I know well: that of theological seminary. The academic study of theology is a good thing, a gift of the Creator. It is a thing to love, revel in, and find delight in. So how does it become an idol? Do you know the phrase "iatrogenic disease"? An iatrogenic disease is one which you catch in hospital. You go into hospital with appendicitis and while you are there you catch C-difficile. If you had not gone to hospital, you would not have caught it. In the same way there are diseases that can only be caught in seminary. As Calvin famously said: "[Human] nature is a perpetual factory of idols"—and that factory does not cease production just because someone enters seminary.

1. Warren, "Trying to Satisfy Ourselves," http://rickwarren.org/devotional/english/trying-to-satisfy-ourselves.

So how does studying theology (of all things) carry the danger of idolatry? Surely religious pursuits are immune from such a worldly danger? But the study of theology can become idolatrous in the same way any good thing becomes an idol: when it gets taken from under the Lordship of Jesus and becomes a god in its own right, when it becomes an end in itself rather than a means to the end of serving God more effectively.

I remember a preacher saying, "It was such a thrill the first time I said in a sermon, 'In the Greek it says . . .'" But what exactly is the thrill in this? Is it that if I tell them "the Greek," the congregation will be better equipped to serve God? That is quite possible. Or is the thrill that they will be impressed with me and my learning? Will it help them look through me to God, or will quoting the Greek cause their gaze to stop with me? Is it about God, or about me? If it is about me, it is an idol.

Can idols be redeemed?

What then should be done with an idol? Here is a second shocking statement: God can redeem idols. I do not mean "redeem" in the sense that human beings are redeemed: that through the cross of Jesus our sins are forgiven, we are reconciled to God, and we find our proper place in God's world. Rather, I mean that an idol can be restored to its proper place in God's created order, whether it be our attitude to sex, to material things, to work, or to the academic study of theology.

How does that redemption happen? When those who practice idolatry repent and literally change their minds. They confess, "I realize this thing is not the most important thing in the world, this thing is not going to give me meaning and purpose and identity. This thing is a leaky cistern. What I need is living water! And only God can supply that." As part of surrendering their life to God in Christ, they hand over that idol to the God who made it and who wants to remake it. They take the armor off David and let him be himself—a capable shepherd boy with five smooth stones and a sling.

It may be that Jesus was thinking of Jeremiah when he talked about water. He says to the woman at the well: "If you knew the gift of God, and who it is that is saying to you, 'Give me a drink,' you would have asked him, and he would have given you living water . . . Everyone who drinks of this water [in Jeremiah's terms, the idols] will be thirsty again, but those who drink of the water that I will give them will never be thirsty. The water that I will give will become in them a spring of water gushing up to eternal life" (John 4:10, 13-14).

There is a place in C. S. Lewis's *Prince Caspian* where Lucy and Susan are with Aslan, the lion who is the Christ-figure; and they encounter Bacchus, the god of wine, fertility and theatre (among other things), and a multitude of his followers. He is said to symbolize "everything which is chaotic, dangerous and unexpected, everything which escapes human reason." And a wild party ensues. When it is all over, Susan says, "I wouldn't have felt safe with Bacchus and all his wild girls if we'd met them without Aslan." And Lucy replies, "I should think not!"[2]

Lewis is expressing his deep conviction that everything in creation—including those things which we so easily turn into idols—finds its rightful place only when it comes under the lordship of Christ. Apart from Jesus,

2. Lewis, *Prince Caspian*, 154.

those things are not safe. They can destroy us. With him, they bring life and joy, as their Creator intended.

Scripture: Jeremiah 2.

2

Hedonism

Judy Paulsen

Hedonism and sex have become deeply associated in North American society, but the definition of hedonism actually entails something much broader. Hedonism is the belief that *pleasure is the highest good* in life, whether that pleasure comes from food, drink, sex, stimulating conversation, deep friendship, satisfying work, the fascination of discovery, or the thrill of exploration. Hedonism places the pursuit of pleasure itself as the proper aim of human existence.

Key Questions

It is possible that not many people today consider themselves hedonists. But what does the evidence indicate? One global organization claims it would cost 20 billion dollars to provide clean water to everyone in the world. They also point out that North Americans spend more than that annually on ice cream.[1]

---

1. Voice4Nations. "Water Facts." http://outreach.voicenation.com/water-facts.

"Where your treasure is, there your heart will be," said Jesus. How are we doing at attending to and elevating the great challenges of suffering and injustice in our world? Begin to examine what we spend on entertainment, vacations, and spa treatments, versus caring for refugees or dealing with the problem of human trafficking. Our bank statements suggest that a functional hedonism is alive and well in the more affluent nations of our world. Indeed, we are often quick to defend this behavior. What right does anyone else have to say something about how I spend my money? What right does someone else have to say what is right or wrong for me when it comes to pleasure? If it feels good, do it!

Now if we are honest, part of us can identify with this. We have a sense that if we experience pleasure, that is a good thing. This is so whether we are enjoying a bottle of really good wine, savoring a chocolate fudge lava cake, listening to a beautiful piece of music, or knowing the deep pleasure of human touch. If we *experience* pleasure as good, then surely it must indeed *be* good! And if pleasure is good, why not the ultimate good? If you have only got one life to live then *why not* cram it with as much pleasure as you can?

Scripture's Response

The answer the Bible provides to these questions is that while pleasure is indeed good, if we make it our god then it will be like any other idol. It will eventually consume us, both individually and as a society. This is what the Bible comes back to again and again about idols: they consume us, both individually and corporately. So whether alcohol, sex, money, work, music, or even family or friends become god to you, then they will consume you.

We see evidence of this devastation every time we turn on the news. We learn of a politician who at the height of his career lost everything because of sexual appetites that had come to rule him. There are people whose marriages are destroyed by alcoholism or workaholism. There are those who have become consumed by their pursuit of the latest luxury car, mountain bike, or iphone. There is an alarming percentage of society that now faces serious health dangers due to obesity. There is a growing percentage of young men so addicted to pornography that it is interfering with their forming normal, healthy relationships. All of these tragedies point to how things that started out as pleasures can actually become gods that rule us.

Holiness

From its earliest beginnings, and certainly growing out of its roots in Judaism, Christianity has called its members to practice *holiness* in response to hedonism. But do not look for a rule book. Holiness calls for something that can plainly be called purity. The Oxford dictionary defines the word "pure" as "being of one element," as in pure gold or a pure musical tone—in other words, unpolluted by other things.

Sometimes in the history of the Church, purity came to be equated with chastity, but the Bible itself paints a much bigger picture when it refers to the purity of holiness. It challenges us to be pure by being made up of, and focused on, one thing: loving God, in all the areas of our lives.

The Bible essentially outlines three depths of holiness. At each level there are questions we can ask ourselves, as individuals and as a society:

1. The first level of holiness involves our *actions*. At this level as Christians we ask, "Is *this behavior* something that pleases God?"

2. The second and deeper level of holiness involves our *motives*. At this level followers of Christ ask, "Do *my thought life and my ambitions* please God?"

3. The third and deepest level of holiness involves our *character*. Here Christians ask, "Does *who I am* please God?"

The three levels are inextricably linked, of course. So while being a follower of Jesus means learning how to be holy in your actions, ultimately God wants to have the same effect on your motives and character too.

The Path to Holiness

We live in a culture that resists any constraints on the pursuit of personal pleasure, something that was also true of the Israelites in and around 750 BC. It was a time of extravagant indulgence, immorality, judicial corruption, and oppression of the poor. This was also the time of the Old Testament shepherd-prophet Amos, whose message then was about as popular as it would be today. He writes: "Alas for those who lie on beds of ivory and lounge on their couches and eat lambs from the flock and calves from the stall; who sing idle songs to the sound of the harp, and like David improvise on instruments of music; who drink wine from bowls, and anoint themselves with the finest oils, but are not grieved over the ruin of Joseph" (Amos 6:4–6).

The critique of Amos was that the people were caught up in a functional hedonism that meant they now "were not grieved over *the ruin of Joseph*," a euphemism for the kingdoms of Judah and Israel falling into moral and ethical decay. They had stopped caring about the things God cared about, like injustice.

Just as in the time of Amos, today we are again compelled to ask: How can we resist hedonism? What is the path to holiness? According to the Bible and ancient Christian practice in the life of the church, there are three stepping stones on the path to holiness:

- The first of these is *self-examination*. This involves examining your thoughts, words and actions against the embodiment of holiness shown to us in Jesus our Lord.
- The second is *confession and repentance*. This entails admitting where you have fallen short and turning back again to the right path.
- The third is actually *walking in that path* of God's ways, as apprentices of Jesus Christ.

Perhaps as important as these steps, however, is the recognition that holiness is something we need to hunger for and actively pursue.

Scriptural Insights

In Paul's letter to the Colossians, he writes, "Put to death whatever in you is earthly" (Col 3:5). He describes things like "anger, wrath, malice, slander and abusive language," and says these need to be the things we have "stripped off" as part of the old self, having "clothed yourselves with the new self, which is being renewed in knowledge according to the image of its creator" (Col 3:10). So in order to grow in holiness, we often have to leave behind old ways. Hedonistic indulgences like pornography, gossip, excessive drinking, sexual immorality, foul language, stinginess, and greed have no place in the lives of Christians. We need to avoid these things like the plague.

But we also need to nourish ourselves with those things that will strengthen and grow us in godliness. In his letter to the Philippians, Paul writes: "Whatever is true, honourable, just, pure, pleasing, commendable . . . think on these things" (Phil 4:8). Likewise, in Ephesians we read, "be imitators of God and live in love . . . find out what is pleasing to God . . . Live as children of light . . . and be careful how you live" (Eph 5:1–16). Be careful how you live; that is, live in a counter-cultural way. This precept is reiterated by so many of the biblical writers. Peter wrote, "As he who called you is holy, be holy yourselves in all your conduct" (1 Pet 1:15). Live justice and compassion, to the extent that it significantly impacts your bank account. Further, James, the half-brother of Jesus and head of the church in Jerusalem, wrote, "Draw near to God and He will draw near to you. Cleanse your hands and purify your hearts. Don't be double-minded any longer" (Jas 4:8).

Conclusion

Peter Kreeft, professor of philosophy at Boston College, writes in *Back to Virtue* (1992): "A pure will loves God with the whole heart and soul and mind. It is the greatest compliment a lover can give: I love you with my whole heart and soul. My love is not divided. You have no rival."[2] May God, by His Spirit alive and at work in us, lead us ever deeper into a holiness based in such a love as this.

Scripture: Amos 6:1–14.

---

2. Kreeft, *Back to Virtue*, 173.

3

Narcissism

PETER ROBINSON

OUR WORLD IS A very strange place. All the proof we need that this is a big old goofy world is that presidential candidate Donald Trump said outrageous things over and over again in his campaign. He is a classic example of a person whose ego is out of control. It is all about Donald. And that fits the definition of a narcissist.

Narcissism is an inordinate fascination with oneself, displayed in excessive self-love. Signs of narcissism include grandiose thinking, exaggerated self-importance, a belief that one is special, a need to be admired, and a feeling of entitlement.

While Donald Trump might provide us with an extreme example of narcissism, the broad conditions of narcissism are something we all experience at one time or another. In fact a normal part of growing up is transitioning from the belief that we are the centre of the universe to the recognition that the world is a lot bigger than us. One of my nephews, when he was two or three years old, would arrive at my parents' house. Walking through the front door, he would declare "I'm here," and then he would wait until we all came running—which we usually did. What is normal for a young child is a problem when we get older. Yet there are signs that many of us find it difficult to grow up.

Narcissism cannot be mentioned without reference to the popularity of the selfie. Selfies are not by definition narcissistic, but they do suggest an inclination in that direction. We need only mention what happened in Costa Rica in September 2015. Crowds of tourists were so busy taking their selfies with the sea turtles that they stopped the turtles from laying their eggs. That kind of self-focus is more than a little strange. Another sign that we struggle with this self-focus is the rapidly growing religious category of those who are "spiritual but not religious." That is the perfect religion for narcissism, because it affirms our right to choose a god or gods who fit with who we are.

Image of God

In Genesis we have the declaration that human beings have been made in the image of God. In the church and in the world, we have a long and troubled history of reading this passage as a declaration of our uniqueness and importance. In the process we somehow forget that the focus of the story is God. That we are in the image of God has been understood to mean that there is something about us that is god-like. That is all we have needed to forget God and focus on what makes us so special.

Imagine a gallery opening for an exceptionally gifted artist. The crowds wandering through the gallery talk about the extraordinary vibrancy of the paintings, the rich colors, the evocative images, and most of all the astonishing talent of the artist. After closing that evening the paintings begin talking to each other, delighting in how amazing they are, their uniqueness, and their natural beauty. Eventually they get into arguments over which of them is the most magnificent and the most irreplaceable. They have lost sight of what they are. They have lost sight of their creator.

We live in a beautiful world, yet the result of our self-preoccupation is a hopelessly distorted view of our world, of God, and of ourselves, with all of the consequences that go with that skewed understanding.

Grace of God

Part of God's grace towards us in Jesus Christ, the one who is the true image of God, is that he wants to heal us, to liberate us from the narrow little world of self-preoccupation and self-focus, to enter into the extraordinary world created, sustained, and guided towards its purpose by God.

One of the most practical ways to counter our tendency to self-preoccupation when we are reading the Bible is to always begin with the question, "What does this say about God?" rather than the more typical (and natural) question, "What does this say about me?" When we read the creation story asking what it says about God, we hear that God has created a world that is amazing, complex, beautiful, and good. It affirms how God works in the world and with the world, and it points towards God's intentions for the world. The story of creation does not focus on the uniqueness of human beings, but the generous, gracious, and intentional creativity of God.

God did not create human beings after the seven days of creation. Rather, God created us as part of creation. Our place is in creation, not above creation. Psalm 8 expresses it so clearly when it asks, "What are women and men, that you are mindful of them?" (v. 4). They are mortals, they are flesh and blood like the rest of creation; but you have made them a little lower than God. God has crowned them with glory and honor (v. 5). We have a special place in creation, and we have been given a particular role in relationship to the rest of the world. This is so, not because of who we are, but because of who God is and what God intends to do in the world.

This realization helps us begin to see things in the right order: the world does not revolve around me, it revolves around God. As painful as that recognition might be to a child who has yet to grow up, for an adult it is a great relief because it allows us to begin to make sense of the way things really are. Becoming a Christian does not mean that God is now on my side, but that I am now on God's side. Rather than hoping and praying that God will help us in what we want to do in the world, we are invited to be a part of what God is doing in the world. So we ask and affirm:

> "What are women and men that you are mindful of them? But you have made them a little lower than God and crowned them with glory and honor" (Psalm 8:4-5).

> "O Lord, our Lord, how majestic is your name in all the earth" (Psalm 8:9).

Scripture: Genesis 1:26-30, Psalm 8.

4

Individualism

DAVID KUPP

RECENTLY, THE INTERNET DELIVERED to me the momentous discovery that Frank Sinatra's rendition of "My Way" was the most popular funeral song in our part of the world. This is proof that individualism will never die. A more recent survey by North American funeral directors has discovered that "My Way" has been bumped to second spot. The top funeral song now is Monty Python's "Always Look on the Bright Side of Life." What this is proof of is a legitimate question.

Composing a contribution on "Individualism" as an idol or myth of our age has an inherent irony to it as a task. This essay was written by me as an individual. I talked to no one about it, looked no one in the eyes, and composed it in isolation. Neither was the essay crowd-sourced. A few secondary works were consulted, but in the end not much used. So I write, participating in the high art of ecclesiologically-sanctioned individualism, making me I suppose part and parcel of the "pedagogies of empire." This is all the more reason that we might do well to heed Paul's call to community in 1 Corinthians 12.

According to the biblical scholar James Dunn, the collection of church communities in Corinth "was a very mixed group, with several differing views and practices which put considerable strains on their common life."[1] That is putting it lightly, some might say. Other commentators identify divisions between the ethnic purists and the integrationists; the traditionalists and revolutionaries; the slaves and free; the low-born and the high-born; those with and without foreskins; scandalous social, economic and spiritual divisions; and conflicts over the Eucharist.

Probably for these reasons, Paul is working hard in the last chapters of 1 Corinthians to argue for a sense of cooperation and to describe the great potential of synergy amongst groups of people that were struggling with and angry over their differences. In this respect, 2 Corinthians may indicate that he was partially successful.

Body Imagery

In employing the imagery of the body, Paul is probably borrowing. This language is not unknown among other texts in Paul's world. However, what is striking is that Paul employs the same body imagery but in the reverse direction. Paul uses the body imagery to remind those at the top of the hierarchical pile that the lesser members of the body have a unique and important place in the body, and are to be valued. Do you hear powerful echoes of Jesus here in the gospels? A similar echo of the upside-down Kingdom?

By reversing the use of the body image, Paul challenges the cultural assumptions of hierarchy and authority, and presents an alternate image of life lived in community with God and one another. So there is a political and

---

1. Dunn, 1 *Corinthians*, 9.

an anthropological message here: not only is Paul railing against disunity, he is defining a new form of social and cultural equity within the Christian *ecclesia*. Paul is repeatedly interested in honor and respect across the board, for every single member, whether capable or vulnerable.

Paul obviously was not speaking as a microbiologist, but he nailed it rather well for our twenty-first century sensibilities. Considered as a whole, both the human body and the church are composed of billions of different parts. The human body is miraculously complex with its 37.2 trillion cells, its 35 million heartbeats every year, its 200 billion red cells produced every day, and the fact that there are 100,000 kilometers of blood vessels in each body.

This complexity and the complexity of the global body of Christ are similarly startling and difficult to fathom. Christ's living body today is miraculously complex, composed of billions of members, located in millions of different settings, with thousands of living languages, unique cultures and expressions of the true faith. Multiply this by the complexity of Christian expressions throughout the twenty centuries of this era.

This raises a question: when he employed the body analogy, was Paul thinking about a single fellowship of Christians in Corinth? A number of commentators push the circle wider. No single fellowship, house church, cathedral, in fact no diocese, no denomination can reflect this complexity. The "body of Christ" today is writ large and completely.

Church and Society

In the twenty-first century, in the era of a full planet of people in crisis, in the industrialized, urbanized and globalized human and built ecology we have created, the interpretation and application of this text have gained further ground. Thus, there are black and womanist readings of 1 Corinthians 12, as there are ecological readings of it. There are human microbiota readings here which may help us tackle our aversion to "the other" as found in the foreigner, in the poor, in refugees, and in the vulnerable.

Have we structured our church and society for the wrong kind of individualism? Many of our trends towards hyper-individualism seem profoundly unhealthy. The church may be complicit here, and even causal. The cultural indoctrination towards individualism and the privatization of our faith has been exacerbated by a certain Protestant trend to view faith as a personal relationship between me and God, centred on a person's salvation.

We seem incapable of living without heroes, for we lift them onto pedestals and worship at their feet, no matter how much they reek of clay. We hoist aloft the Obamas and the Trudeaus, and then we give them 100 days to prove they are gods, knowing all the while that crash landings abound. We set up saints, and priests, and scholars, and activists, and CEOs, and authors, and actors, and presidents. We quote them in our papers, our sermons, and our Facebook pages. We admire the lone wolf.

We build education systems that isolate students and evaluate them as lonely self-contained entities of knowledge and skills and behaviors. We set each other up for failure, because we cannot speak openly and without fear of our *angst*, and our weaknesses, and our disagreements, into the space Paul calls the body of Christ. Our wealth and urbanized individualism is also generating an increasing loneliness as we climb late at night up to condominiums in the sky, in urban spaces where we know none of our neighbors.

Search for Home

It seems as if there is nothing wrong with individualism, and there is everything wrong with individualism. We are fragmented, postmodern urbanites. One minute we are off to the shops, then onto the subway to catch a concert, then 20 km across town to work, then back the other way to the gym, then 25 minutes north to a house group, and finally "home." Whatever "home" is. Is it the place where the last time we talked to a neighbor was in January? In identifying the overlaps (or lack of them) between the people and communities at each of their nodes of life, in many cases we find few if any overlaps in the patterns of their lives. There is no synergy as individuals rocket endlessly between unconnected towns on a train line.

Paul would be astonished at our urban fragmentation, which daily drives us speedily apart under the power of hydrocarbon fuels. "How can you know anything about the body of Christ," he might ask us, "if you have structured life for zero synergy across your many communities, both physical and virtual? What can you know about Christian formation? How can you practice discipleship, mentorship, coaching, and apprenticeship in The Way if you have built and structured everyday life to prevent it?" How can you endure suffering, without having built resilience? How can you experience common and deep joy, without a common and continuous, multi-dimensional experience of life?

Community

It may be helpful to recast our hyper-individualism and to view it as the "arrested development" of our era. In following Richard Rohr or Carl Jung, we can think of individualism as a stage of life to grow out of, into deeper interdependence and community. But I wonder. Unless we understand and begin to counter postmodern urban fragmentation, can our many attempts at parish building, at community development, at justice for the vulnerable, at transformation of systems—can these activities be more than water through the sand? Unless we find ways to practice Paul's reversal of community from the bottom up, our activism, our teaching and preaching, our discipleship are co-opted by the individualism captured within top-down politics, top-down mercantilism, and top-down ecclesiologies.

So where does this leave us? Paul says, "Now there are varieties of gifts, but the same Spirit; and there are varieties of services, but the same Lord; and there are varieties of activities, but it is the same God who activates all of them in everyone" (1 Cor 12:5–6). There is one Spirit but a variety of ways that people work for transformation. For some, this will mean a passion for peace; for others, a passion for political liberation. For some, it will mean a passion for life and its sacredness; for others, a passion for forgiveness and mercy. For some, a passion for tight interpretations of the Scriptures; for others, a passion for a more radical contextualization of the text. For some, a passion for evangelism; for others, a passion for justice. All of these people are working for the common good of the upside-down Kingdom. Each is inspired by one and the same Spirit, the Spirit who gives to *each* person their unique and different *charisma*.

Finally, remember that when we leave this text, and move on to 1 Corinthians 13, Paul outlines a more excellent way. That is, if we do not have love inside us for the other, for our sisters and brothers who think and feel differently than we, we are nothing. The greatest *charisma* that God has for us is love. Love for people who do not think, believe, or live like us. Love for people who do not share our point of view. Rather than becoming individualists and heroes, we are to make love our goal, our aim, and our greatest purpose in life.

Scripture: 1 Corinthians 12.

5

Consumerism

L. ANN JERVIS

BY THIS POINT IN the gospel of Luke, Jesus has been revealing in word and deed the nature of what he brings to Israel and through Israel to the world. He is the one in whom God is again reaching out God's saving hand—the one who is God's salvation, a light to the Gentiles and the glory of Israel.

Immediately before this passage, Jesus has declared to his disciples the absolutely critical nature of acknowledging and accepting who he is: "I tell you, everyone who acknowledges me, the Son of Man will acknowledge before God's angels. But the one who rejects me will be rejected before God's angels" (Luke 12:8). Then someone standing in the crowd that surrounds Jesus and his disciples calls out, "Teacher, tell my brother to divide the family inheritance with me" (Luke 12:13). Jesus's response to the man in the crowd clarifies again who he (Jesus) is, what he is among them for, and what he offers those who would see and hear. "Friend," Jesus says, "who appointed me as a judge or referee between you and your brothers?" (Luke 12:14).

Here, in classic Jesus fashion, Jesus changes the agenda. In effect he is saying: "You, friend, may know me to be wise and just, but my business is not about settling your family squabbles. My job is to go deeper than that. My business concerns your heart, your desires, your deepest motivations—your life. I am among you in order to transform your very being—in order to give you access to true life."

Jesus commands the man in the crowd. Using the imperative mood, Jesus says *orate*, meaning "watch carefully"; and then he uses another imperative, *fulassesthe*, that is "avoid or be on your guard against" *pases pleon exias*, i.e. every kind of covetousness.

Then Jesus makes plain that he does not see covetousness as just a bad thing and that he is not regarding it as a disposition and activity that contravenes a law, although, of course, it does contravene one of the Ten Commandments. Rather Jesus directly takes the matter of covetousness to another level. He says, "Watch intensely and be on your guard against every kind of covetousness because your life does not consist in the abundance of possessions" (Luke 12:15).

Jesus goes on to give a parable to illuminate the level he wishes his hearers to know and enter. It is the level and the reality he lives and knows: the world of life, the cosmos that God controls, and the reality Jesus has been seeking to open up to his hearers all along.

Jesus gives the parable of the rich man who became even richer and whose only thought was how he could satisfy himself with his wealth. The man who, when he saw the abundance of his crops, asked *himself*: "Oh, what shall I do, I have no place to store my crops" (Luke 12:17).

This was the man who did not think about sharing his plenty, the one for whom Jesus's idea of selling his possessions and giving to those in need (Luke12:33) did not occur. This was the man who could not imagine a life like Jesus describes immediately after this parable: a life of desiring only God's kingdom and trusting God for what we eat and wear.

Jesus tells the parable about the rich man who became richer, who did not think about feeding the hungry with good things, and who did not think about using his abundance to bring good news to the poor. He did not think of his riches in light of God but only in relation to himself.

The rich man in the parable is blind to the reality Jesus lives and opens up: that life is in God and only in God. Jesus illustrates the myopia of this man in a scene that would be laughable if it were not so tragic, the scene when the man ponders what to do about his wealth not by talking with God, but to his own soul. "Psyche, Soul," the man says, "soul, you have ample goods laid up for many years: relax, eat, drink, and be merry" (Luke 12:19). This rich man sees his riches only in the context of the tiny world of himself, and this blindness is his poverty, in fact it is his death. That night, God demands his soul from him. Jesus closes the parable by saying, "So it is with those who store up treasure for themselves but are not rich towards God."

Consumerism is, of course, the fuel of the Western economy. Consumerism relies on covetousness—on believing that having things, perhaps especially having more things than someone else, will bring us life.

I am not sure what you think of Rousseau, but on this matter I believe the Enlightenment thinker was wise. With the rise of consumerism, Rousseau saw a society based not on egalitarianism but on envy.

I expect many of us might agree. Using the words of Jesus: consumerism incites every kind of covetousness. The challenge that disciples of Jesus have is not normally that of recognizing this; the challenge is rather how to avoid being drawn into consumerism and so into covetousness.

Paul knew something of the challenge of covetousness. In Romans 7 he uses the example of the commandment against coveting to describe the challenge of the Christian life. Sin can use even the good commandments to produce the very thing we are commanded not to do. Paul knows that the law reveals sin but that it cannot defeat or control it. He writes: "I would not have known what it is to covet if the law had not said 'You shall not covet.' But sin, seizing an opportunity in the commandment, produced in me every kind of covetousness" (Rom 7:7). Paul ends the chapter with the cry: "Wretched man that I am, who will save me from this body of death?" (Rom 7:24). And then he answers: "Thanks be to God through Jesus Christ our Lord!" (Rom 7:25).

It is Jesus who saves us from the poverty, indeed from the death that comes from every kind of covetousness. Today he gives us the commands that—unlike following the law—allow us to participate in our salvation from coveting. Jesus, through his person among us, enables us, encourages us, empowers us to *orate* and *fulassesthe*—to watch intensely and be on our guard against every kind of covetousness.

Jesus, because he is God's salvation among us, can help us to protect ourselves against the illusion that having stuff will give us life. It is Jesus who has taken us to that other level—to what is real and true—Jesus who can free us from coveting, and who opens our eyes to the life of God which is our treasure.

Scripture: Luke 12:13–23.

6

Omnism

Joseph Mangina

According to the Oxford English Dictionary the word omnism, derived from Latin *omni* or "all," was first used in 1839 by the otherwise forgotten poet Philip J. Bailey (1816–1902), who wrote "I am an omnist and believe in all religions."[1] Nowadays the word is used more broadly to denote a pluralistic approach to spiritual matters, one that opposes strict dogmatic formulations, and that seeks harmony and agreement among religions rather than discord. The omnist, then, is neither theist nor atheist, but a kind of all-theist. This raises the inevitable question: is omnism true? The answer is, No.

As an intellectual position omnism is hardly worth the time we would spend refuting it. There are a hundred questions one might ask of omnism, but perhaps the most basic is, how would you know? How would you really *know* that Christianity and Buddhism, say, are really saying the same thing, or that different religions offer up fragmentary truths that we can pick like so many flowers

---

1. "Omnist, n.," *OED [Oxford English Dictionary] Online*, Oxford University Press. http://www.oed.com/view/Entry/131259?redirectedFrom=omnist.

from a field? Where do you stand when you say something like that? Surely not within Christianity or Buddhism themselves, each of which has a very particular vision of what it means to be human and of what the fulfilment of human existence looks like. For the Buddhist, the self is fulfilled when, by ardent training and practice in adherence to the excellent Eightfold Way, all desire ceases and there is no more self to suffer; this condition is known as Nirvana. For the Christian, the self is fulfilled in a life of faith, hope, and love in obedient discipleship to the Lord Jesus Christ, consummated by the eternal vision of the Holy and Blessed Trinity.

We might also think of the different roles Buddha and Jesus play for their respective followers. In Buddhism, Buddha is the greater teacher of the way to truth. In Christianity, Jesus *is* the Way. These pictures of what it means to be most fully human are as different as chalk and cheese. That does not mean that the Buddhist and I have nothing in common, that we may not learn from one another, that we cannot live together as neighbors in a pluralist society, etc. All it means is that each of us has deep convictions that go so far down that we would not easily trade them in for the other's. If there are things Buddhists and Christians share—and given that we are both human and, from a Christian perspective, creatures of God, it would be surprising if we do not—then these must be discovered by patient exploration. The well-kept secret about interreligious dialogue is that it is very, very difficult hard work.

The omnist, then, is able to affirm all religions by adopting a position safely above them. He treats religious truths like so many options on the menu at a fast-food restaurant. "Have it your way," they say at Burger King. It is a quintessentially postmodern attitude toward truth.

Omnism says that it values all faiths, whereas in reality it devalues all of them, treating them as so much raw material for one's own spiritual project. This is why omnism is—not to put too fine a point on it—an extremely boring creed, no match for the extraordinary story that begins with the words "In the beginning God created the heavens and the earth" (Gen 1:1) and concludes with "even so come, Lord Jesus!" (Rev 22:20).

But you see, what I have just done is fallen into the trap that awaits any writer who dares to relate the gospel to contemporary culture. The trap is that in relating Christian faith to "*isms*," we will begin to talk about the "-ism" more than the gospel. Worse than that, we will attack the "-ism" from a secure standpoint of knowing that we are in the right and others are wrong. This is not a very biblical outlook. The problem with Baal, for example, is not that the Canaanites worshiped him but that Israel did. So too with omnism. The problem with omnism is not that all those footloose individualists out there want to believe anything and everything. The problem is that *we Christians* want to do that—not as an intellectual position, either, but as the foundation for a whole way of life. It is we who want to follow Jesus *and* have our middle-class lifestyle, follow Jesus *and* have a successful career—maybe even a career in the church?!—follow Jesus *and* maintain our pet ideology or political program or scheme for saving the world, the way the Galatians thought they could worship both Christ and the elemental forces of the cosmos. Who are the omnists? We are the omnists, the people who never saw a both/and we did not like. In the immortal words of Pogo: "We have met the enemy and he is us."[2]

2. Kelly, *Pogo*.

What will save us from our omnism? Neither we nor our theological critique of omnism, necessary as that may be. The only One who saves us from our self-constructed idols is the Lord God, whose coming is announced in Isaiah 48. The word "monotheism" fails to do justice to these latter chapters of Isaiah, in which the church has always heard the strains of the gospel. Not just *that* there is one God, but that the Lord himself comes among us, is Isaiah's message. The Lord comes, putting the world on notice that he will not tolerate any rivals:

> Listen to me, O Jacob,
> and Israel, whom I called!
> I am he; I am the first,
> and I am the last.
> My hand laid the foundation of the earth,
> and my right hand spread out the heavens;
> when I call to them,
> they stand forth together.
> Assemble, all of you, and listen!
> who among them has declared these things?
> The LORD loves him;
> he shall perform his purpose on Babylon,
> and his arm shall be against the Chaldeans
> (Isa 48:12–14).

This is the gospel. This is the good news. This is the coming of God. This is the terrible swift sword of His either/or, putting an end to the hopeless compromises of our both/ands. When God comes, the idols flee away. The good news is that omnism is not our fate. So next time you are tempted to bow down before an idol, remember who you are. You are a Christian. You do not worship all gods but the One God, Creator of heaven and earth and the Father of our Lord Jesus Christ. He is the original iconoclast, smasher of idols, and he has come to set us free.

Scripture: Isaiah 48:12–22.

7

Fatalism

Christopher Seitz

The people caught up in consumerism, individualism, narcissism, and hedonism are enjoying themselves. Take away the negative labels, and one can sense the allure, even if they are corrosive over time and certain to bring a hangover.

But fatalism does not have this same aura. It seems more obscure and darker, for it is difficult to think of many happy fatalists. Once in Scotland I shared a hospital room with a bona fide Free Presbyterian who not only believed in election but knew himself to be elect. He did seem to enjoy this status, fated to be saved. But I have never met anyone like him before or since.

Pursuing an *interpretation* of fatalism or the spiritual disease that animates it, one recalls the man who for thirty-eight years sat by the pool at Bethsaida. He told Jesus he could not wash there because people got in front of him, or pushed him aside. Thirty-eight years is a long time. That must feel like fate. Fatalism is like the disease the monks called the noonday devil. Or it is like the voice of despair expressed in such phrases as: "Who cares?" "What's the point?" "I'm stuck." "Here we go again." "It's no use." "Time ain't on my side, no it ain't."

The passage in Isaiah is often held to describe fatalism. "I am the Lord, and there is no other. I form light and create woe. I am the Lord who does all these things" (Isa 45:7). You there, sit by a pool for thirty-eight years. You over there, collect $38 million in a lottery. I form light, I create woe. I am the Lord who does all things.

These verses from the forty-fifth chapter of Isaiah have been so read. But that would make them stand in sharp contrast to otherwise triumphant chapters. For Israel is in despair. She is stuck in time. The idol-isms that marked sinfulness and avoidance of judgment have crashed to earth. Full judgment has brought its curtain down. Kings murdered, people deported, land forfeited, temple gone, and sacred memories shattered. "She has received double for all her sins" (Isa 40:2), the prophet announces.

It is into just this state of affairs that the prophet cries with energy, "Comfort, comfort my people, speak tenderly to Jerusalem and cry to her, that her warfare is ended, her iniquity pardoned" (Isa 40:2). Fatalism be gone. "Behold I do a new thing" (Isa 43:19). "Get up, take up your bed, and walk" (John 5:8).

Fatalism is a disease that refuses to pray because God is gone. That cannot escape the gravity of doubt, guilt, conviction of sin, or overriding injustice and spiritual confusion. That these ailments are not all on one page, and some may even be opposites, shows the strength of fatalism's grip. Our divinely inspired prophet counter-punches, because God counter-punches inside him. The silence of despair and fatalism is shattered exactly at the place where it is allowed full voice.

CHRISTOPHER SEITZ: *FATALISM*

If you were asked to name a psalm that most gives voice to despair and fated darkness—and the competition would be strong—the average believer would say, "My God, my God, why hast thou forsaken me? Why art thou so far from helping me, and from the words of my groaning?" (Ps 22:1–2). Far, but also painfully near in absence, in our felt loss of His presence.

There is no book in antiquity or on our shelves today that is more honest about the spiritual despair of the very people God has elected to share his life with. We want to bank the fires of despair, or call them unlucky. Things that will pass as mysteriously as they came. When they are gone, we keep them out of the photo album. But the psalmist asks that his tears be stored in a bottle. His request is granted in the words of these psalms that we recite. And on *this law*, Psalm 1 tells us, the righteous meditate day and night.

What then breaks the spell of fatalism? It is surely the participation in the cries and groans of those who have been faithful before us. Calvin knows that *the godly* are those for whom these expressions of doubt and grief are most real and most true and most healing. How can that be?

Surely it is his knowledge and ours that the Son of God walked into the place of utter fated death and darkness, and joined his voice of forsakenness with every known human instance of that. "He became sin who knew no sin" (2 Cor 5:21). Because it is God's very own self that wills to conquer all that comes between us and him. "Behold, I do a new thing. Created now, and not before" (Isa 43:19). Something never created before: a death with the authority to destroy death. It is a fate, his fate, defeating fatalism. With the power to take up our cries of injustice or proper justice, sinfulness or innocence, entropy or stout rebellion, attack from without and from within, allow them vent, and then say back with final full force, "Behold, I do a new thing." Behold, I make all things new. Get up, take up your bed, and walk. Roll the stone away.

The halls of time are littered with refuse from the work of the noonday devil. Israel's heart and spirit were broken by deserved judgment, a fate that engulfed and overwhelmed. Yet here it is, in just this place, where God promises to do his best work, for those who cry out and put their trust in his final power to declare and to make all things new.

> "Remember not the former things,
>
> nor consider the things of old.
>
> 19 Behold, I am doing a new thing;
>
> now it springs forth, do you not perceive it?
>
> I will make a way in the wilderness
>
> and rivers in the desert.
>
> 20 The wild beasts will honor me,—those hedonists—
>
> the jackals and the ostriches—O consumerist—O individualist—
>
> for I give water in the wilderness,
>
> rivers in the desert,
>
> to give drink to my chosen people,
>
> 21 the people whom I formed for myself
>
> that they might declare my praise (Isa 43:18–21).

Scripture: Isa 43:16–25.

8

Careerism

THOMAS POWER

OCTOBER 2015 MARKED THE six hundredth anniversary of the victory in 1415 of King Henry V of England over the French at the battle of Agincourt. Not the least important aspect of that victory was the performance of the English fleet, consisting of fifty ships. Either pietism or militant religiosity informed the naming of Henry's ships. His four greatest ships were the *Trinity Royal*, the *Grace Dieu*, the *Jesus*, and the *Holigost*. All the rest were named after the Virgin Mary, the three persons of the Trinity, or various saints.

As God's servant, Henry felt it was his duty to forcefully implement what he thought was God's will. On one occasion, in the wake of slaughtering every male over the age of twelve in a French city, Henry informed a Dominican friar who took him to task over the massacre that he, Henry, was the "scourge of God, sent to punish God's people for their sins." While Henry might justify such acts of terror, so concerned was he to secure his standing in the afterlife that he ordered thousands of masses to be said after his death. Yet his reign as a king was deemed a success. We might say that he had a very successful career with an impressive résumé filled out with military achievements and demonstrations of religious fervor.[1]

Paul wants us to pay attention to similar features in his own background that he identifies as common to people in general. Paul's résumé was impressive. He too had the background that seemed to guarantee career success in the eyes of the world. He lists seven résumé highlights, four based on birth, three based on achievement. Thus circumcision, racial and tribal origin, and Hebrew lineage were the credentials that provided him with claims of social status, legal standing, and security that collectively formed the basis of his relationship with God. To these pedigree attributes he adds three more résumé features based on his strict adherence to the laws, zealous persecution of Christ followers, and a blameless record in following the law, that together pointed to personal career achievements. These highlights of Paul's impressive curriculum vitae show that his pedigree and achievements were the basis of his life. He depended on them for a right relationship with God. Together they all added up to what he calls collectively "a confidence of the flesh" (Phil 3:3).

But then Paul had a life-changing encounter with Jesus Christ. After that, claims of heritage and achievement counted for nothing. They could no longer be the basis of security and confidence. They were just outward forms. He calls them rubbish. They were a barrier to being in a true relationship with God.

He is not saying that in and of themselves his background and achievement lacked merit. It is just that they gave a false security and a confidence of the flesh that came in the way of a real relationship with God made known in

1. For the foregoing details see Keys, "What's in a Name?," 7. https://www.churchtimes.co.uk/articles/2015/16-october/news/uk/what-s-in-a-name-a-clue-to-fervent-royal-religion.

Christ. He now has a right relationship with Christ based on faith, not on all his previous qualifications or claims to special status. That relationship is now based not on what Paul can do, but on what God in Christ has done that is certain and secure.

Confidence of the Flesh

Like Paul, the phrase "confidence of the flesh" aptly summarizes what our culture mandates as security. "Confidence in the flesh" can sum up a career that brings success, status, respect, and wealth. These are the collective elements that constitute careerism, whose relentless pursuit is sanctioned by our culture. If we place reliance on them as our main source of security and identity, derived from our own achievement, then they lead to competition and jealousy with others, and other sinful tendencies.

More importantly, because they assume idolatrous status, they compromise the faith we should have in Jesus. They become the marks of our own attainment, identity, and security; then as idols, they substitute for faith in God's grace and provision as demonstrated in Jesus Christ.

This realization raises such questions as:

- What then are we to think?
- What is legitimate in terms of career?
- Where does the line of demarcation lie between legitimate ambition and achievement, and the idolatry of careerism?

Career and Vocation

For a start, we need to distinguish between vocation and career. A job is a job. But vocation comes from God, gives us our identity, and coheres our gifts and talents, our personalities and temperaments to a divine purpose.

Second, in contrast to careerism, which is predicated on self-fulfillment, vocation calls us to consider areas of need in the world where we might help or serve. In identifying such needs, we look to God's Word and the leading of the Holy Spirit. If we follow our calling we use our gifts to make a difference in the world.

Careerism brings with it the seduction of power, excessive desire for material security, and the longing for status, choices Jesus faced when tempted in the desert (Matt 4:1–11; Luke 4:1–13). A life lived with career at the centre is one based on a confidence in the flesh. What differentiates vocation is that it is a life fully committed to Jesus that brings glory to God.

Conclusion

There is some of Paul and King Henry in all of us. Perhaps we do not subscribe to their religious fanaticism, but certainly inherited features of race, ethnicity, and nationality, as well as a sense of our own achievements, may be influential. Paul is saying that such attributes do not matter. They are real, but they do not give us any status before God.

So let us cast aside the idolatry of a life based on confidence in the flesh. Instead let our ambition be to dedicate ourselves in faith, service, and obedience to the work God has called us to in the world.

Scripture: Philippians 3:2–11.

9

Relativism

MARION TAYLOR

RELATIVISM SUGGESTS THAT ALL viewpoints are equally cogent and that all truth is relative to the situation, individual, group, or culture that constructs the truth. Relativism has become part of the warp and woof of our pluralistic post-Christian culture. It has also invaded Christian culture. Pope Benedict XVI spoke eloquently about the threat of relativism: "We are moving toward a dictatorship of relativism which does not recognize anything as for certain and which has as its highest goal one's own ego and one's own desires." Unlike the Christian faith that is based on the creed of the church, he suggested, the pervasive philosophy of relativism that appears to be "the only attitude acceptable to today's standards" involves "letting oneself be tossed and swept along by every wind of teaching."[1]

Contemporary society is not the first to embrace a philosophy that tells us there is no right or wrong. The time of the judges in the Old Testament was also such a time, as "in those days there was no king in Israel, everyone did what was right in his own eyes" (Judg 17:6, 21:25).

1. Pope Benedict XVI, "Pro Eligendo Romano Pontifice," homily at the Vatican Basilica, April 18, 2005.

The period of the judges was a time in the history of God's people when God's law was more often than not ignored, when life was lived without reference to moral absolutes, and when there was no king. In Judges, we witness a cycle that repeats itself over and over again as Israel turns from God to moral relativism, a move that leads to disaster, despair, and God's judgment. The book of Judges can in fact be read as a manual for what happens when a society adopts a philosophy or ethic of moral relativism: an ethic that most often leads to disaster and collapse. It is an ethic which the narrator of Judges equates with evil (Judg 2:11).

The story of the Levite's concubine and the debacle which follows it in Judges 19–21 puts a human face on moral relativism. The story begins with a Levite from the hill country of Ephraim taking a concubine from Bethlehem who leaves him and returns to her father's house.[2] Four months later, the Levite tries to persuade her to return home. One night during their journey home, the couple finds themselves without shelter until an old man offers them hospitality. He warns them of the dangers of spending the night in the open, but these dangers follow them back to the old man's house as the men of the city surround it and demand sex with the Levite. The men of the city refuse the old man's offer of his virgin daughter and the Levite's concubine. The Levite pushes his concubine outside, where she is raped and abused throughout the night. At daybreak she falls at the door, where she lies until the Levite opens it, demanding that she get up. When she gives no answer, he places her on his donkey, returns home, dismembers her, and sends her twelve body parts to

2. This summary of the story draws on the introduction to nineteenth-century discussions of Judges 19 in Marion Taylor and DeGroot, eds., *Women of War, Women of Woe*, 244–45.

the various tribes, demanding that action be taken against those who caused her death.

When the tribes learn what happened they are disgusted, and under the direction of the Levite mount an attack against Gibeah. The Benjamites, refusing to attack their fellow Israelites living in Gibeah, respond by defending Gibeah; and a bloody battle ensues, killing thousands of Benjamites and destroying their towns. Four hundred virgins from Jabesh Gilead are spared to become wives for Benjamites who survive the slaughter, while six hundred men who still need wives abduct girls from Shiloh as they dance at an annual festival.

This story in Judges is arguably the most poignant example in the Bible of what happens when God's people abandon the notion of moral absolutes and do what seems right in their own eyes. This story is seldom read or talked about in church. Its literal sense is clear, as it shows that life without a king—life without law, order, and structure, and without God—leads to disaster: it leads to chaos and the final demise.

For many interpreters throughout history, the plain sense of the story of the Levite's concubine was too revolting to read or talk about. Nineteenth-century free-thought writer Annie Besant (1847–1933), who spent her life arguing against traditional moral absolutes, simply acknowledges the sordid nature of the story, describing it as "the horribly disgusting tale of the Levite and his concubine."[3] Anglican commentator Mary Cornwallis (1758–1836), however, engages the horror of the concubine's plight and voices her strong disapproval of the actions of the men in the story. They should have "defended life and honour to the last," instead of making "such a horrid compromise

3. Besant, *Woman's Position according to the Bible*, 3.

with monsters in wickedness."[4] In her final comments at the end of the book of Judges, Cornwallis addresses the recurrent problem of human sin, tracing a grim picture of salvation history beginning with Adam and continuing to the present. She concludes: "but every effort of Infinite mercy, to secure the happiness of mankind, has been in turn abused or rejected, and nothing remains, within the limits of Divine justice, but a separation of the righteous from the wicked at the last awful day of general judgment."[5] When everyone does what is right in their own eyes, the moral collapse of society and God's judgment follows.

Cornwallis agrees with the conclusions of Archbishop James Ussher (1581–1656), who placed blame for the "many horrid things" and unpunished offences committed by "every tribe, every city, [nay] and every private man" on "the want or lack of a supreme authority." He suggests that the lesson of the book of Judges is that we should "be thankful for the authority which is set over [us], to preserve [us]" from the consequences of relativism.[6]

Nineteenth-century evangelical social activist Josephine Butler (1828–1906) agrees with Ussher's and Cornwallis's reading.[7] But Butler goes further to find in the story's darkest scenes God's message for her world. She fuses the horizons of the original story and the present, reading it as a story about women who are trafficked, and those who either victimize or ignore them. She feels called

---

4. Cornwallis, *Observations*, 361–2. For a full discussion of Cornwallis's treatment of this story, see Taylor and DeGroot, *Women of War*, 246–48.

5. *Observations*, 367.

6. *Observations*, 364.

7. For a full discussion of Butler's interpretation of this story, see *Women of War*, 248–57.

by God to challenge the rampant moral relativism in the church and society.

As part of her address before four hundred women whom she was trying to recruit to support the campaign against the Contagious Disease Acts in 1870, Butler rehearsed the story of the Levite's concubine. Butler's retelling of Judges 19 focuses on the "ghastly details" of the story—"the clamouring of the sons of Belial round the door, the suspense, the parley, till, in the cowardice of self-defense, the man brings out that helpless woman, and casts her among the hellish horrors of that awful night."[8] Butler discloses her hermeneutical approach when she describes this story as one of the "many tragical histories recorded in the Old Testament, that true mirror of the faith and the righteousness, but also of the depravity of man." She calls attention to the poignant parallels between the abuse of the concubine and the situation of contemporary prostitutes, declaring, "there is a weak and prostrate figure lying at our door; to this door she turns for help." She also reads the story within its larger canonical context, using such intertexts as Luke's story of Jesus being anointed by the immoral woman of the city who perfumed and kissed his feet and then experienced Jesus' forgiveness (Luke 7:36–50), Revelation 3:20 ("Behold, I stand at the door, and knock"), and the story of the woman with the issue of blood touching the hem of Jesus' garment (Luke 8:40–48), to bring Jesus into the story of the rape of the Levite's concubine.

To the poignant theological question, "Where is God in the midst of this horrific story?," Butler answers that Jesus is there at the door with the concubine. Not surprisingly, Butler concludes her sermon with a call to her audience

8. For Butler's 1870 address based on Judges 19, see Butler, "The Lovers of the Lost," 16–19. She also published her thoughts on this topic in 1898, "A Typical Tragedy," 111–14.

to extend their love to fallen women, outcasts, and sinners, as they too are made in God's image. Her experience of working with prostitutes had shown her that most prostitutes were themselves victims. She de-emphasizes the depravity of the prostitutes, stressing instead the depravity of the moral relativists who did what was right in their own eyes by valuing prostitutes as less than fully human and unworthy of love, acceptance, and even redemption.

The story of the Levite's concubine brings us face to face with the dangers of moral relativism. In his groundbreaking book, *The Gospel in a Pluralist Society*, Lesslie Newbigin declares "the relativism which is not willing to speak about truth but only about 'what is true for me' is an evasion of the serious business of living. It is the mark of a tragic loss of nerve in our contemporary culture. It is a preliminary symptom of death."[9] Josephine Butler had the courage to face the serious business of living in Victorian England. Her reading of the story inspires us to recognize the evils in our own day and to stand up against them. As Christians, we are called to challenge the relativism that screams at us at every turn. Like Butler, we need to have the courage to challenge relativism's message that there is no right or wrong, because we know that there is right and wrong. Thinking otherwise is what God's people did in the time of the Judges; and as the story of the Levite's concubine reminds us, such a philosophy of life leads to chaos, death and judgment.

Scripture: Judges 19:1–6.

---

9. Newbigin, *The Gospel in a Pluralist Society*, 22.

10

Gnosticism

Glen Taylor

I LOVE WORDS AND especially odd things about how they are spelled. Take for example the fact that "gnosticism" is spelled with a "gn" but is pronounced as if it began merely with an "n." As with the word "gnu," a word for an antelope-like animal, it is not pronounced "g-n" as the "g" is, of course, silent. Who would have "gnown"?

The gnostics were an ancient group popularized today as those lying behind some of the non-canonical gospels, such as the Gospels of Judas, Thomas, and Mary. Long before the discovery of these additional so-called gospels, the ancient church father Irenaeus wrote about the gnostics. Yet, partly because of our society's insatiable appetite for what is new and different, these later, less-reliable gospels have captured more attention than they deserve through the publicizing efforts of such people as Dan Brown (author of *The Da Vinci Code*) and Elaine Pagels. However less appealing it might seem, the truth remains that late and likely derivative "gospel" writings ought not to be taken more seriously than early, ubiquitous and pristine ones!

Gnosticism and the Bible

The New Testament scholar Norman Perrin characterizes Gnosticism as follows:

> For most Gnostics, humanity is intrinsically good, in fact consubstantial with the divine. But, after being created, humanity falls back into a protracted stupor; it forgets its divine origins and is tricked by the malevolent creator into thinking that there is none higher than the creator. Taking pity on humanity, the true God then sends the Redeemer figure down through the heavens in order to reveal knowledge and thereby to awaken the divine spark within humanity. Those who recognize this divine inner spark have secured their redemption, proved themselves among the elect, and transcended the evils of material creation.[1]

We need to add to this summary the notion that gnostics in general believed that spiritual things, like our souls, are inherently good and thus important and valuable. Conversely, material things like the world and our bodies are inherently bad and of little value. In view of this, the world in which we live, being a material thing, cannot according to the gnostic have been made by the supreme God. Thus, the God of the Old Testament, as creator of the world, must have been some low-ranking junior god.

But since the Old Testament existed at the time of the gnostics, how did they respond to claims found in the Old Testament such as Isaiah 45:5, where God says: "apart from me there is no God"? To the gnostics, this kind of claim

---

1. Perrin, "Gnosticism," 257.

"only betray[ed] his peevish arrogance and ignorance of transcendent reality."[2]

And what do the gnostics claim about Jesus? He was sent to blow the whistle on the junior god of the Old Testament who made the world and whose minions continue ineptly to perpetuate the messy tangled web of material existence. And, given the gnostic aversion to the material, Jesus occupied only what seemed to be a human body, which he left just prior to his crucifixion. (Gnostics claim it was Simon of Cyrene who was on the cross.)

In response to such ideas, a website (gotquestions.org) put it well by saying: "Such views destroy not only the true humanity of Jesus, but also the atonement, for Jesus must not only have been truly God, but also the truly human (and physically real) man who actually suffered and died upon the cross in order to be the acceptable substitutionary sacrifice for sin (Heb 2:14–17)."[3]

Gnosticism Today

The spark of gnosticism still flickers today. Take for example the idea that knowledge, especially new knowledge discovered by a particularly gifted individual, is valuable, even redemptive. Might our thrill over new discoveries in some way reflect the sense of salvation that gnostics evidently felt when they gained new and privileged "insight" that the divine spark lit within them? Might there also be something gnostic in our love to be in on a secret that allows us to form *here* an "us" group in relation to *there* a lesser "them" group? For example, a former Methodist I

2. Ibid., 258.

3. "What Is Christian Gnosticism?" https://gotquestions.org/Christian-gnosticism.html.

know describes his move to Anglicanism as "seeing the light" and "coming of age." Each of us, regardless of what denomination we belong to, can do this, as can those who shun or transcend denominational affiliation. In short, there is something gnostic in many of our claims to privilege owing to special insight.

Or think of an implication of the current hype over the gnostic gospels. Elaine Pagels, for one, claims that the gnostic gospels testify to a commendable diversity of Christian belief that prevailed within Christianity during the first few centuries.[4] By stressing this supposed wide diversity attested by the gnostic writings, Pagels and others welcome theological diversity, including extreme forms that were once regularly termed "heresy." Some advocates of the new "Pelagian orthodoxy" regard traditional orthodox Christian belief as none other than the product of narrow and fanatical "heresy hunters" who straitjacketed Christianity into a single doctrinal framework.[5] As one reviewer puts it, Pagels leaves "the impression that everything about Jesus and the Christian faith is up for grabs" and thus, by implication, everything should be up for grabs today.[6]

In general, however, those gnostic texts that convey obscure ideas are entirely lacking in the sort of historical pedigree that can be traced forward from the much earlier and more reliable canonical gospels. The same reviewer quoted above sounds a welcome note of calmness and sobriety in reaction to the hype over the gnostic gospels

4. See Jones, "The Gospel of Judas," http://www.thetruthaboutdavinci.com/the-gospel-of-judas-two-levels-of-scam.html.

5. See, for example, chapters 4 and 5 of Elaine Pagels, *Beyond Belief: The Secret Gospel of Thomas*, New York: Random House, 2003.

6. http://www.thetruthaboutdavinci.com/the-gospel-of-judas-two-levels-of-scam.html.

when he writes: "The 20th century Church was not taken by surprise in 1945, when 52 Gnostic texts were found in Nag Hammadi, Egypt. [And the fairly recent discovery of the Gospel of] Judas is not 'explosive.' *It merely brings the count to 53.*"[7]

Psalm 111

Psalm 111 strongly contrasts with the gnostics' diminutive view of Israel's God by ascribing to Him dignity and honor. Psalm 111 affirms the glory, majesty and holiness of Yahweh, who makes provision for (and by implication has created) the worldly order. His daily dealings in this material world are normal and right, and in no way reflect the mundane dealings of some junior god who, having created a bungled world, elicits the aid of angelic lackeys for crisis management. Rather, the supreme God of Israel does splendid deeds that reflect his qualities of truth, justice, and equity. According to verse 9 it is Yahweh (the creator) who sent redemption his people's way. His name is holy and merits respect. He is gracious and compassionate. Orthodox Christians take these biblical claims about God for

---

7. Ibid. Emphasis mine. Jones continues: "Perhaps we should apply a 'hermeneutics of suspicion' to scholars like Ehrman and Pagels, both once evangelical Christians, who, favoring their own theological and spiritual relativism, pounce on these recently-found texts to frame the issue, grab the headlines, and produce a preposterous account of early Christianity. We are asked to believe that one of the most successful religious movements in the whole of human history began with radical confusion and mind-boggling uncertainty. Gospels like Judas are only 'gospel' for scholars like Pagels since such confusion means that 'Christians' today can believe anything they want with a clear conscience. Pagels herself chooses a blend of Christianity and Buddhism and admits that she finds herself strangely drawn to Gnosticism" (ibid.).

granted, yet they sharply contrast to the view of this "god" held by the gnostics.

The psalm makes a further claim about God that contrasts with the gnostic view. Contrary to their claim involving "secret" knowledge, the true knowledge of God is public and widely accessible. Our psalmist thus says in verse 1 that he will thank God in the company of others, and that he and the community of faith enjoy tracking his feats. This matter of disclosure extends even to the best-known Old Testament word "hallelujah," which, significantly, is always plural in Hebrew. God's message of salvation has been made known openly to his people through the testimony of the Old Testament prophets and others, including (later) the apostles. This testimony also includes the New Testament Scriptures, which to be such, had a pedigree that extended back to the apostles and that included widespread transmission.

Psalm 111 is a far cry from that of the lone gnostic who whispers secret claims of "true divine knowledge" in our ears. Gnosticism is all about secret knowledge, whereas biblical faith is a matter of public testimony.

The Psalms and Christ

As the rich history of Christian exegesis attests, the Psalms can be seen to point to Christ.

One way of seeing Christ in Psalm 111 is by comparing it with the psalms that immediately surround it. It is immediately preceded by Psalm 110, which Jesus used to support his claim to be more than the son of David by being his "Lord." And Psalm 111 is immediately followed by a psalm that, like a twin, invites comparison with it. For example, both these hymns are rare acrostics; that is, their lines follow a pattern set by the successive letters of the Hebrew alphabet. Also, both psalms begin with the same words and end with a wisdom saying. They are of similar length—79 and 72 words respectively—and share a startling array of similar words or phrases: "delight," "fear," "righteousness," "give," "be remembered," "steady," "upright," "Praise Yah" (in the first line), and "enduring forever" (twice in each psalm). Yet—and here is the point—their similarity isn't what one (especially a gnostic) would expect given the subject matter of each; one psalm is about God whereas its twin is about a human being.

The connection between these two psalms becomes all the more telling upon examination of a few details. In Psalm 112 the man begins the psalm by pronouncing a beatitude, "blessed is the one who . . . ," which welcomes comparison with Another's Beatitudes. Moreover, just as it says in Psalm 111 that God is "gracious, and compassionate" so it says in 112:4 that this man is "gracious, and compassionate" and "righteous." So startling is this attribution in Psalm 112 of what characterizes Yahweh in Psalm 111—being gracious, righteous, and compassionate—that one version of the Septuagint (followed by the Revised Standard Version) adds the name Yahweh to make Him, not a human, the subject of 112:4. Yet this doesn't solve the problem, for 112:6 claims of the ideal son of man: "for unto eternity he can never be shaken; and as a memorial, he shall be righteous to eternity." The tension persists in 112:9, which states of our ideal human figure: "His righteousness stands forever; his horn shall be exalted in glory." Given the fact that David speaks in Psalm 110 of a surprising new figure who is Yahweh's vice-regent, one who rules from Zion with a scepter issued by God, and who is a priest forever after the order of Melchizedek, Psalms

111 and 112 read like an elaboration upon this mystery individual, claiming in essence that the spoken-of human in Psalm 112 is an incarnate form of Yahweh as described in Psalm 111.

Having noticed the relevance of Psalm 112 to 111, let us return once again shortly to Psalm 111. The word in 111:5 for the "food" that Yahweh has given to his people is almost always used elsewhere as prey from a "kill."[8] It is as though Yahweh planned to feed his flock with the body of a creature, reminding us of Christ's death. In support of this, these psalms together introduce the collection of Psalms (113–118) sung by Jews from ancient times during the Passover, making the parallel line of 111:5, where it refers to "being mindful of his covenant," the act of redemption at Passover, something supported by the later verse which states (v. 9): "He has sent redemption his people's way, and commanded his covenant forever." Moreover, by comparing Psalm 111:5 with its counterpart in Psalm 112:9, it is the righteous individual in Psalm 112 who can be understood to provide the "prey" that God has given to those who fear Him in Psalm 111, such provision being described as a gracious act of "dispersing generously to those in need."

In sum, in addition to Psalm 111 testifying to a God whose supremacy cannot be reconciled with the gnostic understanding of the God of Israel, and in addition to Psalm 111 upholding the truth that knowledge of God is conveyed publicly from among the community of faith over generations, Psalms 111 and 112, following from 110, jointly testify of Yahweh as the one true God who, again contrary to the teaching of the gnostics, was capable of becoming incarnate in an ideal human being. In other words,

8. Our word "know" is related to the Greek word *gnosis*.

things are as Paul said: "God was in Christ, reconciling the world to Himself" (2 Cor 5:9).

Gnosticism is a different religion than that of the Bible. Gnosticism is no substitute for, nor must it ever be associated with, the Gospel. Rather, as Simon Peter claimed in Luke's Gospel, Jesus is the crucified one whom God Himself has declared to be not only Messiah but Lord (Acts 2:36).

Scripture: Psalm 111.

11

Positivism

Alan L. Hayes

Along with our other idols, positivism has an interesting history and a whole set of contested meanings. Here, however, the assertion is made that positivism is the attitude that our only authoritative knowledge is what can be verified from our experience of the natural world, typically through the experimental or empirical sciences.

Many will be familiar with the most famous positivist of our time, the character on Canada's favorite television program, *Big Bang Theory*, named Dr. Sheldon Cooper. He is a theoretical physicist at the California Institute of Technology. Sheldon can explain anything and everything scientifically, and he does not have much respect for any opinions that cannot be supported by science. For instance, in series two, episode nine, Sheldon decides to help his roommate win a girlfriend by having him open a jar with a tight lid, with a great macho show of strength. Sheldon's reasoning goes like this: "When a female witnesses an exhibition of male domination she produces the hormone oxytocin which can create the biochemical reaction in the brain which laypeople naively interpret as falling in love." The point is that a team of scientists can objectively identify and measure biochemical reactions in the brain, but a team of scientists *cannot* objectively identify and measure love, so you can have knowledge of biochemical reactions, but you cannot have knowledge of love, and even to think that there is such a thing as love is a little naive. The challenge that this approach poses for people of faith is that, since God can never be the object of scientific experimentation, the positivist views the idea of God as strictly meaningless.

To counter this, one could simply quote Scripture and show how wrong this point of view is. Specifically, one could quote the passage, "Although you have not seen Christ, you love him; and even though you do not see him now, you believe in him" (1 Pet 1:8). Scripture says that there are significant realities, in fact ultimate realities, that you cannot see, but you can and should believe in them.

Complexities

That may be largely true as far as it goes. But things are more complicated than that, for "–isms" such as positivism *do* usually contain truths. In fact, most "–isms" are truths that have been taken to extremes; they have gone totalitarian on us; and they have been allowed to clear out other truths that are actually at least as important. This means that there is a danger in simply wagging our finger at "–isms," calling them idols, and getting rid of them. If we could succeed in doing that, we would risk getting rid of the seeds of truth that they contain. But we could not succeed in doing that anyway, because "–isms" are pretty firmly embedded in the worldviews that we have been socialized into.

Moreover, "–isms" are not really a threat to the gospel. They fall under their own weight. Positivism is kind of a joke. That is the basic premise of *Big Bang Theory*. The two main characters are opinionated nerds who hurt people without knowing it and are pretty oblivious to justice, beauty, and social skills. They are objects of fun. A recurring humorous theme in the television series is that, although they have a fond belief that science is true and religion is superstitious, their science really *is* a form of religion. They are *theoretical* physicists, after all, which means they cannot really prove any of the theories that they are so strongly committed to, and they have passionate disagreements about things no one can know for sure. Some positivists on the program are totally certain that biology explains everything and some are totally certain that physics explains everything, and they argue bitterly about who is right. Some are sure that string theory is true and some are sure that loop quantum gravity theory is true, and disagreements like that can break up relationships.

Humility

As with our stereotypes of religious fundamentalists, the positivists on *Big Bang Theory* have very little humility as to what they cannot know. In one episode Sheldon's roommate, Leonard, finally loses his temper about something that Sheldon did and tells Sheldon: "The worst part is that you don't even understand what you did wrong because you can't conceive of anything that you're not an expert in." To which Sheldon replies: ". . . 'anything in which you're not an expert.'"

Another positivist of our time, but this one a real one, is Richard Dawkins, a famous atheist, who has made a lucrative career of being self-assured in pronouncing that religion is simply a social meme. He made up the idea of social meme, and this is an idea that is even harder to prove than God. A lot of scientists think that social memes are pseudo-scientific nonsense. But criticism does not daunt Richard Dawkins, whose humility is on the same level as Sheldon's and Leonard's.

Building Bridges

People of faith need not be scared of positivism; but what if we go further, and say that it can actually be, in fact has actually been, an instrument of blessing? We should perhaps aim in this direction if we think that the main message of the gospel is not condemnation, but redemption. That is, what if our job as Christian disciples is not to condemn positivism, but to appropriate it for the gospel?

When Pope Francis returned to Rome after his visit to Cuba and the United States, he said something in his first speech in St. Peter's Square that summed up his trip, and summed up his ministry and the mission of the Church, and maybe the whole gospel of Christ. He said: "It is God who builds bridges; we build walls." Some popewatchers are now summing up Pope Francis' ministry by calling him "the bridge builder." His point is that walls do not work. We try to wall off difficult relationships, we try to wall off the dark pieces of our souls, we try to wall off dangerous ideas, and we try to wall off parts of Scripture that bother us, but none of that quite works. The more we build walls against other things, the more we build walls around ourselves that trap ourselves inside. God wants to build bridges. Discipleship is about building bridges.

Confronting the Idols of Our Age

So what if we build bridges to the other "-isms" considered here? What would that look like? While individualism can go too far, the gospel does make a claim on me, the individual, and calls me to work out my own individual salvation in fear and trembling. Careerism goes too far, but God does call us into a vocation which has real importance in God's plan. Fatalism sounds bad, partly because the fates of Greek mythology are not as personal as Jesus Christ, but the idea that we fit into a purpose that was created for us long before we were born is true to our faith, and it is comforting to know. As long as these principles are not seen as master truths that explain everything else, as long as they can be seen in the context of the gospel, they are not idols, but wisdom.

What does our bridge to positivism look like? Here is an idea. One hundred years ago, Albert Einstein gave the lecture in Berlin that proved the theory of general relativity, by explaining a shift in the orbit of Mercury that the laws of gravity could not account for. He demonstrated that space and time, which we experience as different, are really one thing, and although we experience them as stable and predictable, they are not. That subverted the idea that any scientist has the capacity to observe the world as it is. Since then, what scientists have discovered about the structure of nature has moved farther and farther from what we experience and from anything that might pass for common sense. There are sub-atomic particles that can exist in two distant places at once. There are black holes. You cannot observe the building blocks of reality as they are, because observing them changes them. Randomness is built into nature. David Eichler, a theoretical physicist in Israel who is also a religious Jew, told a reporter, "As we know from quantum mechanics, the laws of physics proclaim their own incompleteness, and that leaves, as one logical possibility, plenty of room for God to intervene."

So positivism, in the history of thought, has done a great service. Beginning with positivist principles and following experimental science as far as they can go, scientific researchers have demonstrated the impossibly of having an empirical knowledge of the world as it really is. Gravity is true to our experience; the warping of space-time by mass is not. The positivists have brought us from thinking of the universe as a great big clock, all very mechanical, very predictable, impervious to divine intervention, understandable without any need for divine revelation, to realizing that the structure of nature is an unfathomable mystery with plenty of room, at every moment, for God's grace to work. Scientific reality turns out to be utterly vast in its diversity and utterly beyond human comprehension.

From that discovery, people of faith can experience ourselves as encountered by the amazing handiwork of a sovereign and loving God, and from there we can be led into prayers of thanksgiving for the miracle of grace that we have a place in it. So we can allow ourselves to be led "to rejoice with an indescribable and glorious joy" (1 Pet 1:8).

Scripture: 1 Peter 1:3–12.

12

Reductionism

Ephraim Radner

Reductionism means taking something complex, rich, and textured, and explaining it in such simplistic terms as to be able to manipulate it, control it, own it, and finally dismiss it. For example: claiming that religious faith is really certain synapses in a particular part of the brain, firing a certain way. Or that human society is a set of economic relationships of exploitation. That is reductionistic. Not only does it obscure the reality in question, it denies the work of God. Here I want to provide a reductionist proposal to expose all reductionisms.

The proposal I have concerns all the "-isms" of our culture, that is the idolatries associated with individualism, narcissism, consumerism, relativism, and so on. My proposal is this: Get rid of email. Actually, go down the line and get rid of it all: yik-yak, twitter, texting, facebook, email, telephones, and TV. They are all satanic.

This is a serious proposal and in making it I am not alone. Philosophers, social commentators, researchers, are saying similar things. Witness the recent bestseller by Sherry Turkle, an MIT professor, called *Reclaiming Conversation*, an anodyne title, but actually concerned with

Ephraim Radner: *Reductionism*

the demise of family empathy due to the smartphone. Yes, satanic: bit by bit, with each one of these contraptions that has become a part of our lives, we have built up and become enmeshed in a culture where the reality of human *being*, face to face, has disappeared. It is satanic, because we are absolutely enslaved to this distorting and destructive prison. We cannot escape. We even invent grand narratives of excitement and awe about each new step in the process, as if we were inventing cures for cancer. All the while we are grinding down the glory of our human createdness as *people*.

It would be appealing to me to say I will not communicate with you except face to face. It would be nice to advocate for digital-free zones. But that would be unrealistic, for there is much good that is being done through educational resources online, for instance, and good people doing it. It would be like getting rid of credit cards; necessary business would fall apart. Still, imagine what the end to this enslavement would look like: obviously, all that wasted verbiage, abstracted ideas, pointless business, false productivity, empty self-expression and vain self-referral, context-less ideation, floating imagery and untethered desire, all of which uphold, in fact, the "-isms" of our day in their particular form and grasp. These would all wither. Instead, we would have to face each other, look in each other's eyes, engage embodied responses, watching frowns, apprehending confusion, enjoying smiles, retreating from or turning towards tears. We would look in those eyes, and through their windows into that great shaft that travels up and down from one infinity to another, and that represents the human soul of another person.

Then and only then would we think and speak, because in fact we would touch flesh and spirit both, the very living stuff by which God has granted us knowledge and self-expression in this place—this tangible world of dust, dirt, ribs, and the rest, which is what a person is, made by God (Gen 2).

Reductionism is simply any and every tendency, slippage, and failure to do just that. In Amos, we learn of those who eagerly "sell the needy for a pair of shoes" (8:6). In Revelation, we have this kind of thing, talked about throughout the Old Testament, brought to its conclusion: "The kings of the earth who have committed fornication, shall bewail her . . . saying, 'Alas, alas, that great city Babylon . . . for in one hour is thy judgment come.' And the merchants of the earth shall weep and mourn over her; for no man buyeth their merchandise any more: . . . gold and silver . . . fine linen . . . Marble . . . cinnamon . . . frankincense . . . beasts, and sheep . . . and the bodies and souls of human beings" (Rev 18:9-13). The bodies and souls of human beings, sold as merchandise. There you have it. That is our world. Meanwhile, the angels in heaven await to see such a world crumble, so that women and men can be treated as God created them to be treated.

One could say, in relation to all the idols of today's "-isms," just what we like to say about sin: that we should hate the sin, and love the sinner. "Hate the '-ism,' love the '-ismer': or 'love the -ist.'" I hate narcissism, but I love narcissists. Surely that is a start. As a kid growing up in the 1960s and 1970s, I was overwhelmed by the way we were putting people into boxes, one ideological gift-wrap after another, and then throwing the packages at each other with the labels "pig," "commie," or "fascist." Things are now worse at the university level, what with the use of terms such as essentialist, homophobe, postmodernist, hetero-normativist, logo-centrist, and so on. By all means, we must love them as human persons. But there is more. If we truly love, it is only because we love human beings—our "neighbors"—*as ourselves* (Lev 19:18; Matt 22:39). The Marxists or anti-Marxists, or gnostics or anti-gnostics, consumerist or anti-consumerist—they are human beings, because and insofar as we too are like them and of them, and bound up with them, in a single and fundamental way. We too are bodies and souls, trembling before God, tottering on the edge of our creation and our deaths. We have to look at each other to figure that one out and be faithful with its reality, sit in the same room, eat the same food, hear the same voices, hold the same babies, take the same chemo, and touch the same flesh.

We *have* to do that. It is what it means to be bound up with Jesus Christ himself: hearing him with our ears, seeing him with our eyes, touching him with our hands (1 John 1:1). And He us, first of all! To do that with someone does not mean you have to agree with them, or approve of what they do. Indeed, standing before God, that could never be. Only God is faithful; our approvals and agreements are meaningless. But we have to be in the same room, engaged with one another, to figure that out fairly and truthfully. Every "-ism," like racism itself, is founded on the practice of segregation, denying the "like ourself" reality of human createdness by isolating it from the truth that is wrapped up in being "children of men," as the King James Version puts it—translating the "children of Adam," as God looks down on them at Babel and after (Gen 11:5)—*together*, bound to one another as our brother's and sister's keeper. Christianity's claim regarding the Two Adams, the First and the Second, in whom in some real fashion all of us are located in our beginning and ending, is profoundly culture-shattering and life-giving.

For if we look into the eyes of another, whether narcissist, consumer, gnostic, humanist, secularist, universalist or Pelagian, we will see our own eyes staring back, filled with the yearning call to move from First to Last, from my birth, to my death, to God—please, at least that. That is what it means to *be* a human being first of all: one *beggar*, looking into the eyes of another beggar, one beggar talking to another beggar. We are all beggars. This realization messes up all our certainties, and leaves room only for God's One Certainty.

The Church is filled with wonderful things from the past; but we should never look back with nostalgia to the times when Catholic and Protestant (and Protestants among themselves) would not talk or enter the same building; or when Europeans, Indians, and Chinese eyed each other across chasms of alienated judgment. Sunday is still the most segregated day of the week for Christians, with, in North America alone, 80% of congregations made up of homogeneous groups, measured by common social indicators: same race, education, culture, income, age, music preference, and politics. But God has been pushing us, over the centuries, confusing as it may be, into "as your-selfness" —beggars just *as yourself*—pushing us into, not our segregated certainties, but into Christ Jesus, the One Man, the One Human Being for all human beings, souls and bodies. That is His soul, his body. It is our only touchstone, because it is our future.

Only as we are thus pushed into the same room, from the same Adam into the One new Adam, can we get beyond our reductions and actually do something, as D. T. Niles put it: two beggars, looking at the same God, because that is who we are, what we have been *rightly and truly* reduced to. But *then*: One beggar telling the other beggar where to find food, in Niles' famous description of evangelism.[1] Only when we are in the same room can we rise up, take someone else by the arm—flesh to flesh—and lead them to something that both of us are ravenous for, breaking it apart in your hands, placing it in the hands of the other. Being fed—not alone, not apart—but, human bodies and souls that we are, *being fed by God together* (Exod 16:32; Mark 6:34ff). That is gospel, that is truth, and that is grace.

Scripture: 2 Chronicles 5:1, 6:12–37.

---

1. See Black, "The Callings," 38.

Bibliography

Benedict XVI. "Pro Eligendo Romano Pontifice." Homily at the Vatican Basilica, April 18, 2005. http://www.vatican.va/gpII/documents/homily-pro-eligendo-pontifice_20050418_en.html.

Besant, Annie. *Woman's Position according to the Bible*. London: Freethought, 1885.

Black, David. "The Callings." *New York Times* (May 11, 1986) 38.

Butler, Josephine. "The Lovers of the Lost." *Contemporary Review* 13 (1870) 16–19.

———. "A Typical Tragedy: Dead Hands upon the Threshold." *The Storm Bell* 10 (1898) 111–14.

Cornwallis, Mary. *Observations, Critical, Explanatory, and Practical, on the Canonical Scriptures*. 2nd ed. London: Baldwin, Cradock & Joy, 1820.

Dunn, James D. G. *1 Corinthians*. New York: T&T Clark, 2004.

Jones, Peter. "The Gospel of Judas: Two Levels of Scam." http://www.thetruthaboutdavinci.com/the-gospel-of-judas-two-levels-of-scam.html.

Kelly, Walt. *Pogo* [comic strip]. Post-Hall Syndicate, 1949–1973.

Keys, David, "What's in a Name? A Clue to Fervent Royal Religion." *The Church Times* (16 Oct 2015). https://www.churchtimes.co.uk/articles/2015/16-october/news/uk/what-s-in-a-name-a-clue-to-fervent-royal-religion.

Kreeft, Peter. *Back to Virtue: Traditional Moral Wisdom for Modern Moral Confusion*. San Francisco: Ignatius, 1992.

Lewis, C. S. *Prince Caspian*. New York: Collier, 1970.

Newbigin, Lesslie. *The Gospel in a Pluralist Society*. Grand Rapids: Eerdmans, 1989.

Bibliography

"Omnist, n." *OED [Oxford English Dictionary] Online*. September 2016. Oxford University Press. http://www.oed.com/view/Entry/131259?redirectedFrom=omnist.

Pagels, Elaine. *Beyond Belief: The Secret Gospel of Thomas*. New York: Random House, 2003.

Perrin, Norman. "Gnosticism." In *Dictionary for Theological Interpretation of the Bible* (DTIB), edited by Kevin J. Vanhoozer et al., 256–259. Grand Rapids: Baker, 2005.

Taylor, Marion and Christiana DeGroot, eds. *Women of War, Women of Woe: Joshua and Judges through the Eyes of Nineteenth-century Female Biblical Interpreters*. Grand Rapids: Eerdmans, 2016.

Turkle, Sherry. *Reclaiming Conversation*. New York: Penguin, 2015.

Voice4Nations. "Water Facts." http://outreach.voicenation.com/water-facts.

Warren, Rick. "Trying to Satisfy Ourselves." http://rickwarren.org/devotional/english/trying-to-satisfy-ourselves.

"What Is Christian Gnosticism?" https://gotquestions.org/Christian-gnosticism.html.

List of Contributors
(All members of the faculty,
Wycliffe College, Toronto)

John Bowen
Professor of Evangelism

Annette Brownlee
Chaplain, Professor of Pastoral Theology
and Director of Field Education

Alan L. Hayes
Bishops Frederick and Heber Wilkinson Professor
of Church History

L. Ann Jervis
Professor of New Testament

David Kupp
Professor of Pastoral Theology

Joseph Mangina
Professor of Systematic Theology

Judy Paulsen
Professor of Evangelism, Director of the Institute of Evangelism

List of Contributors

Thomas Power
Adjunct Professor of Church History, Theological Librarian

Ephraim Radner
Professor of Historical Theology

Peter Robinson
Professor of Proclamation, Worship and Ministry

Christopher Seitz
Senior Research Professor

J. Glen Taylor
Professor of Scripture and Global Christianity

Marion Taylor
Professor of Old Testament

www.ingramcontent.com/pod-product-compliance
Lightning Source LLC
Chambersburg PA
CBHW070059100426
42743CB00012B/2590